Hygge

IN THE EARLY YEARS

Bringing the Danish approach of warmth,
simplicity and wellbeing
into your teaching and home life.

KIMBERLY SMITH

Hygge in the Early Years

Hygge is a Danish approach to life that focuses on living in the moment and enjoying every minute. It's not about having to buy new things but simply taking the time to appreciate and enjoy the special every day moments we have.

This book aims to take you on a Scandinavian journey which will focus on regaining your work life balance and also learning how you can create a calmer and more purposeful approach to your teaching and leadership in the early years. Take time reading the book and give focus to the slow and gentle approach on reflection this offers.

The features of this book include;

- High quality colour photographs for inspiration
- Practical suggestions for managing your own work life balance
- Guidance on creating your own hygge inspired classroom
- Example of embracing in the moment planning
- A guide for managing transitions across the early years day
- Suggestions for how you can appreciate hygge moments throughout the year
- Bonus E-Content to see Hygge in action

Written by an international Early Years consultant, trainer and teacher, this book provides practitioners with practical ideas and suggestions for bringing a little bit more calmness and appreciation into your day.

Kimberly Smith is an experienced Early Years teacher and leader and now shares her knowledge and inspiration with others. Working as an international Early Years consultant and writer supporting schools, settings and childminders. Through her extensive travels of Scandinavia she has developed a lifestyle that appreciates all things hygge.

Contents

1	**Introduction**	4
	What is hygge? 7	
	Wellbeing 11	
	Stress and anxiety 12	
	Wellbeing in young children 13	
2	**Hygge in the Early Years**	15
	Time and timetables 19	
	Transitions 21	
	Learning environment 25	
	In the moment planning 33	
3	**Hygge at Home**	41
	Food 40	
	Home made 48	
	Vitamin D 55	
	Interiors 58	
4	**Early Education for Sustainable Development**	60
	Introduction 60	
	Environment 63	
	Social and cultural 67	
	Economic 70	
5	**Leading in the EYFS**	79
	Meditation 80	
	Apps 81	
	Appreciation 82	
	Hygge Office 82	
6	**Hygge through the Seasons**	63
	Winter 84	
	Spring 86	
	Summer 87	
	Autumn 91	
7	**Bibliography and Photos**	95

Introduction

The UK is currently experiencing a severe teacher shortage and alongside this the amount of trainees applying for teacher training places has dropped significantly year on year over the last 5 years. It is estimated that for every 10 teachers required there are only 8 teachers to do the role. Now this book isn't going to spend time looking at the reasons for this. I think anyone working in schools already has an idea of the increased workload, paperwork and scrutiny the profession is working with.

As a teacher, leader and consultant myself I have seen both first hand and in others how weeks, days and hours are counted down each term till the next holiday. Teachers knowing that for those two weeks at Easter they can switch off from work and feel an improvement in their own wellbeing.

Yet this isn't good enough. We can't be seen wishing our days away and losing belief in ourselves that we can't do our job. As leaders in the classroom our mood and wellbeing is transferred down onto everyone we come into contact with. So if we are feeling worried, over worked and tired our children will pick up on this and they too will have a lower level of happiness. We need to promote children's self belief that they can do something and spread enthusiasm that will inspire life long learners. I know too many great teachers that have left teaching recently or who are seriously considering it. Having almost left myself, my wise words to you would be don't quit. If this is you then take a break, rest, change schools, travel the world. Then make sure you come back and find a school that nurtures, cares and believes in you. Once you have found the right school then you will know it was the right decision to keep on going and you too can make a significant impact to improve the outcomes for children.

With all this going on it's no wonder the UK is often seen at the lower end of the chart for wellbeing and happiness. With many Brits working longer hours and progressing up the career ladder it just shows that happiness is not always linked to success at work. Surprisingly the Scandinavian countries of Norway, Finland and Denmark are top of the happiness chart again in 2017.

With the cold and harsh Scandinavian winters and long dark nights what factors make them so successful at achieving a high level of wellbeing?

The Danish concept of Hygge

Scandinavia ranks highly on all the main factors found to support happiness: caring, freedom, generosity, honesty, health, income and good governance. With the long dark nights they have to have a mind set of positivity. So when it's cold and snowing outside they turn the situation around and light a fire, candles and get blankets. They take enjoyment from the warmth they experience while reading a book by the fire and watching the snow fall outside. This concept around living for now is known as 'Hygge'.

The concept of 'Hygge' (which can be pronounced hue-guh) doesn't have a direct translation into English but a is about embracing the simple moments in life with such joy and appreciation. Whether it be a meal at home with good friends, playing board games or taking time to enjoy a sunny but cold woodland walk.

This isn't an approach that you have to buy into. For instance there are companies out there trying to sell a 'Hygge look Kitchen' or photographs of overly stylish cups of coffee and fluffy socks in blogs and magazines. The whole idea of this way of living is that you don't need anything new or to even spend any money and your house and moments don't need to be magazine worthy. The precious moments in life are right there for you to discover.

This book isn't going to be a quick life fix. You already have the ability to live well and I will just help you to take the time to recognise that. This is all.

Time for reflection

Before we start the course I would like to you to write down all the things that make you happy. Now make a list of all the things that you do each day.

Now make sure you do a little bit of what you love each day!

What is wellbeing?

Wellbeing, mindfulness... two of the words that have gained popularity in use in 2017. What do they actually mean?

Well-being refers to feeling at ease, being spontaneous and free of emotional tensions and is crucial to good 'mental health'. Well-being is linked to self-confidence, a good degree of self-esteem and resilience.

Mindfulness is about living in the moment and Professor Mark Williams, former director of the Oxford Mindfulness Centre describes it as taking the time to know what is directly happening around us and in ourselves. It is crucial for mental wellbeing.

Through increased mindfulness in ourselves we can learn to enjoy every moment more and it fits in closely with the hygge concept. Mindfulness is recommended by the National Institute for Health and Care Excellence (NICE) as a way to prevent depression in people who have had three or more bouts of depression in the past.

Signs of stress and anxiety

- Worrying
- Moodiness and sensitivity
- Feeling over whelmed and unable to cope
- Over or under eating
- Finding it difficult to remember things and focus
- Frequent minor illnesses
- Loss of libido
- Sleep disturbances
- Drinking alcohol more or increasing the amount you smoke
- Physical changes like sweating, headaches, spots, mouth ulcers and a fast heart rate.

Wellbeing in young children

At the Research Centre for Experiential Education at Leuven University, Belgian Professor Ferre Laevers has developed a 5 point scale to measure a child's well-being alongside their levels of involvement.

This scale allows us to see if a child's wellbeing needs are being met by the teaching and provision. We can tune into the child's mental health and consider their emotional and cognitive needs. Over a series of observations a constant level of low wellbeing and involvement leads to low levels of achievement which then impacts on child development. If we see through our observations that a child is working lower than a 4 on the scale then learning will be limited.

The Leuven Scale for Involvement

Level	Well-being	Signals
1	Extremely low	Activity is simple, repetitive and passive. The child seems absent and displays no energy. They may stare into space or look around to see what others are doing.
2	Low	Frequently interrupted activity. The child will be engaged in the activity for some of the time they are observed, but there will be moments of non-activity when they will stare into space, or be distracted by what is going on around.
3	Moderate	Mainly continuous activity. The child is busy with the activity but at a fairly routine level and there are few signs of real involvement. They make some progress with what they are doing but don't show much energy and concentration and can be easily distracted.
4	High	Continuous activity with intense moments. They child's activity has intense moments and at all times they seem involved. They are not easily distracted.
5	Extremely high	The child shows continuous and intense activity revealing the greatest involvement. They are concentrated, creative, energetic and persistent throughout nearly all the observed period.

The Leuven Scale for Well-being

Level	Well-being	Signals
1	Extremely low	The child clearly shows signs of discomfort such as crying or screaming. They may look dejected, sad, frightened or angry. The child does not respond to the environment, avoids contact and is withdrawn. The child may behave aggressively, hurting him/herself or others.
2	Low	The posture, facial expression and actions indicate that the child does not feel at ease. However, the signals are less explicit than under level 1 or the sense of discomfort is not expressed the whole time.
3	Moderate	The child has a neutral posture. Facial expression and posture show little or no emotion. There are no signs indicating sadness or pleasure, comfort or discomfort.
4	High	The child shows obvious signs of satisfaction (as listed under level 5). However, these signals are not constantly present with the same intensity.
5	Extremely high	The child looks happy and cheerful, smiles, cries out with pleasure. They may be lively and full of energy. Actions can be spontaneous and expressive. The child may talk to him/herself, play with sounds, hum, sing. The child appears relaxed and does not show any signs of stress or tension. He/she is open and accessible to the environment. The child expressed self-confidence and self-assurance.

Hygge in the early years

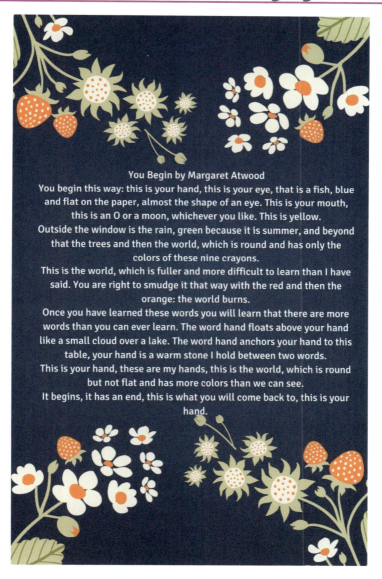

You Begin by Margaret Atwood

You begin this way: this is your hand, this is your eye, that is a fish, blue and flat on the paper, almost the shape of an eye. This is your mouth, this is an O or a moon, whichever you like. This is yellow.

Outside the window is the rain, green because it is summer, and beyond that the trees and then the world, which is round and has only the colors of these nine crayons.

This is the world, which is fuller and more difficult to learn than I have said. You are right to smudge it that way with the red and then the orange: the world burns.

Once you have learned these words you will learn that there are more words than you can ever learn. The word hand floats above your hand like a small cloud over a lake. The word hand anchors your hand to this table, your hand is a warm stone I hold between two words.

This is your hand, these are my hands, this is the world, which is round but not flat and has more colors than we can see.

It begins, it has an end, this is what you will come back to, this is your hand.

With Scandinavia having the happiest people in the world this approach has to start with the children. In Denmark teaching empathy is as high on the curriculum as Literature and Maths. It is woven through the curriculum from preschool all the way up to high school. Not only does teaching about empathy make children more socially and emotionally competent and resilient but it also reduces bullying behaviour. At least one hour a week is set aside for what they call 'Class Hour.' This time is about coming together as a Unit to talk about any problems or worries the children might be having and they discuss solutions together as a group. The teacher's role here is to bring up their own observations of what they have seen each week and support children in recognising and responding to these issues. Each week a rota is in place so that a child from the class will bake a cake and provide it for once the session has finished. During this cake eating time the focus is on togetherness in a relaxing environment where they really do embrace the hygge.

The Scandinavian approach to working in the outdoors that we often refer to as forest schools dates back to the 19th Century. Known as 'skovbørnehaver' (forest kindergartens), 'skovegrupper' (forest or wood groups), 'naturbørnehaver' (nature kindergartens) they too show the importance of developing resilience, self belief and tolerance. The children are also given the space and quietness of the forest environment to socialise and communicate with their friends.

The statutory curriculum in Denmark for the early years must ensure there is planning in place to cover the following areas of the curriculum;

- All-round personal development
- Social development
- Language
- Body and movement
- Nature and natural phenomena
- Cultural expression and values

Visions for the child

When we think about Hygge in the Early Years we are really focusing on the FEELING. What feelings and moments help to drive your practice? What do we want for our children and how will we make sure we achieve this?

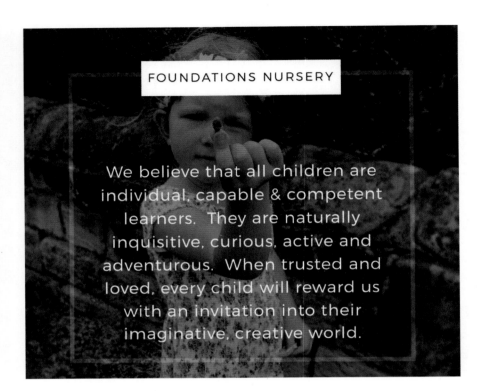

When Lucy and Andy Patrick set up Foundations Nursery in Batley, England they began by asking all staff members to write down their own personal vision for the children. Each staff members contribution was then fed into the overall vision statement and Foundation's nursery was born. This vision now shapes all aspects of teaching and learning from the planning process, the interactions between staff and child and the learning environment.

Time and timetable

Hygge is about leisure and not wanting to rush to get somewhere. This goes hand in hand with our approach for planning. We don't want a tick list approach of adult directed activities a child must get through by the end of the week. We need to be more about the process and not the end outcome. Instead we need to give children the time to learn and play at their own speed. With very young children exploring new concepts for the first time we need to give them time and opportunities to investigate it with all their senses, repeat their experiences and time to explore their new knowledge in different ways. Don't be afraid to slow things down and allow days and weeks to look at a particular concept or idea.

While working in a Bradford school I had a particular group of children fascinated in milk. They were intrigued about where it came from and what we could do with it. Through the children's interest we were able to visit the farm to see where it came from and how a cow was milked, we explored what we could use milk for and made our own cheese and ice cream. We mixed food colouring into the milk and explored colour mixing and pattern making. The learning opportunities that came out of this interest led learning for 12 weeks. We slowed the learning down to give children time to think and process new thoughts and make connections with their new knowledge.

If you're thinking about your daily and weekly time table are you allowing your children long periods of uninterrupted time when they can play and learn with their own agenda? They are not getting broken off to practice their name writing, break time, assembly or to have whole group snack.

Transitions

Alongside timetabling uninterrupted child initiated learning time you might also want to consider transitions around your day. Transitions between activities, to the lunch hall or leaving mum on a morning are times of higher anxiety in young children. We need to reduce the amount of transitions in a day.

The hygge concept is all about moving away from chaotic routines.

Leaving parents on a drop off at nursery or reception is often the hardest part of the session for the child, parents and even teachers. To support this I allow children to access the provision with their parents at drop off time, Children are more likely to be happier about separating from a parent if they are doing something they enjoy. This then allows for the teacher to sensitively interact with the child and parent to have a positive separating experience.

In Norway and Denmark meal times are seen as a time to come together as a unit over some much loved home made food. Yet in England I often visit settings and schools where lunch time feels rushed, noisy and a process rather than an event to celebrate in the day. Not only are young children often fussy eaters but they might be worried about opening their yogurt, leaving the comfort of a familiar room or being with different staff who support lunch time cover. When planning lunch times these factors need to be considered;

- Are the children in a familiar environment?
- Are their familiar adults available to support them and talk to them?
- Does the menu offer a variety of choice across the week? Cooked with seasonal produce.
- Is the lunch time environment calm? Or is noisy, busy, rushed.

- Do children have a regular seat so they always know where to go? One setting I visited recently had a wooden name tag for each child at lunch time at the place setting.
- Could children be involved in lunch time to ease anxiety? Maybe setting the table with a cloth, LED Candles, flowers and knives and forks. Maybe they could write the menu, take orders, serve water and have some responsibility. At Foundations nursery the children bake the dessert each day.

Example of a Healthy Menu for Nursery

Meals	Monday	Tuesday	Wednesday	Thursday	Friday
Breakfast	Cornflakes with whole milk and raisins. Toasted crumpet and spread. Water	Hard boiled egg, whole meal toast, spread and sliced pear. Water	Rice Crispies, whole milk and banana. Water	Malt loaf, spread, plain yogurt full fat. Water	Wheat biscuit with whole milk. Toasted tea cake and spread. Water
Mid-morning snack	Banana and rice cakes Water	Melon, toasted muffin and spread. Water	Strawberries, toasted bagel and spread. Whole milk	Apple, whole meal toast and spread. Water	Sugar snap peas and Hummus Water
Lunch	Beef bolognaise/vegetable bolognaise with white spaghetti. Banana buns Water	Chicken fajita with vegetables and cheese. Berry and fruit flapjack Water	Mixed bean casserole with boiled potatoes and carrots. Apple and sliced pear pudding Water	Salmon and broccoli pasta with sweet corn and peas. Pineapple upside down cake Water	Chickpea and vegetable curry with brown rice Yogurt with berry puree. Water
Mid-afternoon snack	Strawberries and plain yogurt. Water	Breadsticks with Hummus and cherry tomatoes. Whole Milk	White bread with spread Water	Whole meal pita bread with tsatziki and carrot sticks.	Sliced peaches with yogurt.
Tea	Vegetable enchilada. Fresh fruit platter Water	Stirfry veg with a jacket potato. Ginger biscuit and sliced apple. Water	Tuna and sweet corn in pita bread with red pepper sticks. Blueberry muffins. Water	Chicken and couscous salad. Rice pudding with sultanas. Water	Three vegetable omelet (sweetcorn, pepper and peas) Summer fruit crumble Water

Learning environment

Space has to be a sort of aquarium that mirrors the ideas, values, attitudes, and culture of the people who live within it.-

Loris Malaguzzi

When considering or reflecting upon your learning environment it is good to think about the publication 'Early Childhood Environment Rating Scale.' It will take each area of learning and offer a point system for assessing how effective it is for supporting high quality learning experiences.

Another useful point of further reading and research would be into The Communication Friendly Spaces™ (CFS™) Approach by Elizabeth Jarman. This focuses on the role of the environment in supporting speaking and listening skills, emotional well-being, physical development and general engagement. When we use this approach alongside how to create a cosy home the following factors are crucial;

Space and layout

Space to work on a large scale on their own projects with open ended resources. Resources can be transported between areas and encouraged to be used in imaginative ways. Does the space naturally flow? We don't want a reading nook to be in a cold draft or a snack area by the door. Perhaps your snack area could be next to the window to encourage talk about the children's observations of a robin on a tree.

Light

Natural light, cosy light from lamps, fairy lights or LED Candles. We need to avoid the harsh strip lights that often cause headaches and bad moods. Add lighting to your outdoor area on a dull day with LED candles and lanterns. One of my favourite memories of Finland was walking down the street at dusk to see no street lights but candles in the snow instead to guide the way. It was truly magical.

Noise level

Is the space quiet with adults speaking at a level no louder than the children? Not all rooms are acoustically pleasing, especially if there are lots of hard surfaces, so add rugs, cushions and different textures.

Nature

One of the things I love about Nordic homes is their love for caring for plants and herbs inside. Why not add some plants and herbs into vases and pots and display inside? They allow an instant connection with nature. Some of the best plants to have inside are ferns, willows and palms. Display them in interesting pots and containers.

Clutter free

Are areas organised, clutter free and minimalist? Have a sort out and send some things to charity. The environment needs to be well organised and tidy to feel calm.

Calming colours

We are all very familiar now with the natural tonnes of the Scandi house. With hues of grey alongside a white wall. These colours create a feel of calmness as you enter the room. I once worked in a room where all the walls were purple. I think that it sent us all a little bit crazy! Keeping colours neutral allows you to display the children's work on display boards and in frames and it will really stand out.

Warmth

Create a reading nook with blankets, fairy lights and a star projector. Imagine how cosy it would be to cuddle up in there with your favourite book on a cold afternoon.

Avoid ability grouping

How does it make a child at age 3 feel to be put into an ability group for phonics? Grouping in Early Years and Key Stage 1: A necessary evil? Dr Mary Bousted. Is this developmentally appropriate?

Curiosity and intrigue

An environment should promote curiosity and wonder through the interesting displaying of finds and intriguing objects. Do you have a space where you show interesting finds off to others? Get your team looking in charity shops and scrap centres for real objects. Having collections of objects provide lots of natural fascinations for talk and maths. Some of my favourite collections to have are spoons and elephants.

Celebrating everyday moments

Create a diary of highlights with the children. You could ask them what they have enjoyed the most each day and write it down for them and display for parents and carers to see. Discover more online

Spreading hygge into your planning process

Hygge is taking the time to enjoy every day moments. Therefore planning is not helpful when it is done days in advance to a great detail. We can use the elements of the seasons and festivals to create an overview of the year which allows for coverage.

Planning in the EYFS step by step

1. Pick your core stories Plan 6 core stories to focus on throughout the year. One per year. Pie Corbett's talk for writing has many ideas and examples.

2. Select an artist of the half term Select an artist / sculptors/ architect or a type of art to focus on each half term. This could be anything from Islamic art work, David Hockney, Frank Lloyd Wright or Picasso. If you can find a local artist even better.

3. At the start of your year map out your continuous provision plan for both inside and outside. There will be a plan in place for every area outlining the key resources in here. These will stay the same to allow for children to become independent throughout the year in making decisions about what they will do and

take ownership of their own learning. As the year develops you may add other aspects to your continuous provision. For example, higher level joining equipment in your making area.

4. At the start of your year map out a rough guide to enhanced provision for each half term. Planning a rough guide to your enhancements now allows you to ensure you achieve coverage throughout the year and book visits and visitors in advance. We then stick each half terms enhanced provision planning on a larger sheet and add it with other opportunities we have carried out in response to interests. We take a photo of the big sheet each half term before taking it down and add this to our record of planning.

5. Develop weekly planning. This should show coverage across the week of your adult focus sessions. Annotate this at the end of every day to show changes or amendments you have made in response to interests. When looking at your planning for each day make sure you are offering them large periods of uninterrupted time to engage in deeper level child imitated learning. Try to avoid a whole class snack, hall times in the middle of your morning, break times.

6. Establish a weekly rota for your team. This ensures its fair and everyone gets a chance to be outside and shares out the toilet changing too. As a general rule, I do the following for each session; Base Boss- Role is to make sure children are engaged and on task, not wandering around, following the class rules, tidying up and changing children that need it. Adult Focus- An adult that may be working on an adult focus task or interacting with children without being interrupted to manage behaviour or toileting issues. Outside Adult.

Depending on the amount of support you have will determine how this is managed in your setting.

7. Focus child or two This approach is very much inspired from the Anna Ephgrave approach. It just works so well that I had to share. Depending on the size of your group you may select more than one child per week. We organise this so that each child has one focus week over the term. This means throughout the year they will have three. During this time, we use a large A3 Sheet and collect observations on that child each week. We make sure we collect evidence for each area and we also stick photos onto it. When a child is selected for their' special' week they are invited to bring photos and special things in to share with their group. Parents are also given a sheet to fill in. Just to note we collect high quality observations of children all year round and having a focus child a week is additional.

Floor books

Floor books can then be used daily to show the development of a group project and are child led. These might start with a question or idea that the children are interested in.

These can be left out for children to regularly look at and make connections and links with new learning and add to these.

Family Time

Coming together as a unit, family or group of friends is very important as part of the hygge approach and these are the best times. So we need to build this into our teaching approach too.

To embrace the strong focus of the unit and family life we can use our key person groups to create close relationships.

Each day the small key person group can meet with their key person and spend time together talking about things they have done, interested in and planning for the future. This is often quiet time where calming music is played and children show high levels of respect for listening to each other and building relationships.

Wellbeing time

It's very important to build into your day and week calm time for the children that are devoted to their wellbeing. This can be done in a number of ways;

-Small group circle time

-Story massage

There are a series of short routines that can be given on the hand or the back and head. Children offer massage to each other.

The massages are linked to actions in the story. For instance;

Sing a Song of Winter

Sung to "Sing a Song of Sixpence"

Sing a song of winter, (Circle)

Frost is in the air. (Circle)

Sing a song of winter, (Sprinkle)

Snowflakes everywhere. (Sprinkle)

Sing a song of winter, (Sideways Wave)

Hear the sleigh bells chime.(Sideways Wave)

Can you think of anything, (Squeeze)

As nice as Christmas time? (Squeeze)

-Calming music and laying down with a visualization.

-**Yoga**- Why not try reading Ferne Cotton's book: Yoga Babies and encourage the children to join in with the moves. Or perhaps start each day with a yoga session outdoors. Add a Himalayan Singing bowl to start the routine and encourage children to tune into their listening and being present skills. You might add balance boards for an extra level of challenge.

Plan for celebration events

Plan for family celebration events where you can share home made food, children's learning and sing songs and tell stories.

One of the best events I have been part of for families was set in the middle of the woods with a camp fire and live music playing.

Hygge at home

Everything we do in the early years must be for the benefit of the child. If it doesn't have a direct impact then it's irrelevant.

Observations

Are you spending your evenings re-writing your early years observations in your best writing? Try to catch learning in the moment and record it down there and then. Is the importance of the observation that it is in your most beautiful handwriting? If you find it hard writing it down look at an electronic system. I often use videos too to record significant learning moments. This allows me to still interact with the children but capture all of those key moments.

Planning

Adopt an in the moment planning system to allow for flexibility and spontaneity, Often large amounts of time are spent doing very detailed planning in advance that is never looked at.

Email

Turn email notifications off your phone and only check your emails during work time.

Timing

Ever at home and get a message that you're going to have guests in thirty minutes time. The art of cleaning and tidying your house in that amount of time is just brilliant. Now you can apply this method into your every day job list. Set a timer on your phone and give yourself this amount of time to get your work done. When the timer stops you stop too and put the job on your list to finish another day if it's not already complete.

Meal preparation

Batch cook at the weekends with seasonal produce that can be quickly heated up during the week. This allows you to still have time to make meal times special through the week with little effort. You even have time to light a candle and enjoy a glass of wine.

Lunch time as more than a meal

Taking a lunch time at your desk or in your classroom to try and maximise the time spent at work? Constant "productivity" can actually be detrimental to a healthy work-place environment and we end up exhausted and unmotivated. When Scandinavians "break" for lunch, they value the time dedicated to recollecting themselves. It is rare to find people isolating themselves away behind a computer screen when lunch rolls around. Instead, workers leave their desks behind, either to the office cafeteria, or even outside for a relaxing stroll. Lunch time needs to be a moment enjoyed away from the computer screen. See more online!

Outdoor Exercise

Make sure your fit and healthy by taking part in regular outdoor exercise, We feel better when we work out with nature rather than in a gym, Just 20 minutes of walking greatly improves brain activity. Or perhaps you could get on your bike and cycle to work.

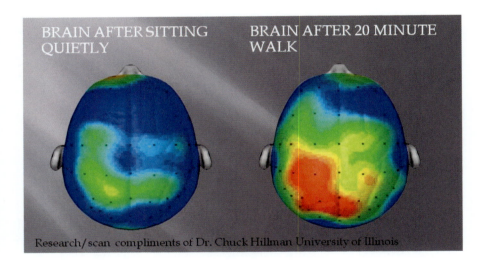

Create a hygge happy playlist

What music instantly lifts your mood when you're having a dull day? For me it has to be a dance around the room to a little bit of Beyonce.

Make time for social events during the week

Have an impromptu BBQ on a summers evening, take part in a pub quiz or have a game of squash with friends. These are all fabulous mood boosters. 'Lykke' which is the Danish search for Happiness focuses on those that are happiest when everyone is equal in a discussion. That means no one person dominates a conversation or brags about their own achievements. Meik Wiking the CEO for the Happiness Institute expresses that when there is a imbalance in equality and fairness divides are created. So forget about bragging about your new designer handbag or shiny new car.

Breakfast

Scandiavians love to spend time by starting the day well. For hundreds of years, porridge has been a staple of the Swedish people. In Viking times, it was the food of the masses, sometimes served at breakfast, lunch and dinner. Now, the first meal of the day is a near-sacred tradition revered for its purity of ingredients and simplicity. In addition to porridge, soured milk, crispbread and open-faced sandwiches with caviar have all been a part of the Swedish breakfast routine. A candle is often lit, napkins used and strong coffee is drank. Don't save your best moments for the weekend.

Bring the outside in

Scandinavian gardens often include purposeful flowers that are grown to be cut and displayed inside. Connections with nature are so important throughout the year.

Seasonal Eating

The best food for our gut is seasonal, fresh and home cooked. During my time in Norway I loved foraging for mushrooms and lingonberries. The berries are then used in juices and jams. Fresh soup is often enjoyed alongside some fresh crunchy bread.

Home made

With the long dark nights through winter don't grumble and complain. Instead light the candles and have a go at crafting. This might be making your own felt Christmas decorations and wreaths or making papercraft. Homemade and home baked goods also make thoughtful and loving gifts.

Making a willow wreath

One my favourite thing to do is make gifts for others. Here is a wreath you can easily create at home for a loved one. Don't save them just for Christmas time either. How about making an autumnal one?

Equipment

- Cutters

- Glue gun

Materials

- 8-10 pieces of willow

- Pom poms

- Wooden shapes

- Buttons

- Hessian Ribbon

- Foliage from the garden; Ivy, Holly, Berries.

Instructions

1. Take a piece of freshly cut willow and carefully bend it round to make a circle. Freshly cut willow is best to use to make sure it doesn't break but is also flexible. Tuck the end of your willow under the edge of the circle to hold it.

2. Take another piece of willow and weave in and out of your first circle with it. Going in and out.

3 Repeat step 2 8- 10 times to build up the shape of your wreath.

4. You could all foliage to your wreath by also weaving that in and out of the willow.

5. Use the glue gun to carefully attach your decorations and a ribbon.

Making Felt Hanging Hearts

These heart decorations look lovely hung around the house throughout the year. I have embraced the Scandi colours in my design but feel free to choose your own.

Equipment

- Sewing needle
- Scissors
- Heart template

Materials

- Felt in colours of your choice
- Thread in complimentary colours
- Buttons
- Lace
- Cotton wool or stuffing
- Card

Instructions

1. Cut out a heart shape out of card and cut it out. This will be your template.
2. Carefully draw around your template onto your piece of felt x 2.
3. Decide on how you want to decorate your heart. You might want to sew a button on the middle or sew other felt shapes onto it.
4. Using a blanket stitch attach the two felt hearts together. Leave a hole at the top.
5. Stuff your heart with either cotton wool balls or stuffing.
6. Use some lace or ribbon to sew a hanger on to the top of your felt.
7. Display around your home or give as a present.

Candle Making

Equipment

- Pan
- Bowl
- Spatula

Materials

- Wax from old candles or wax granules.
- Jam Jar
- Candle Wick
- Scented oil

Instructions

1. Over a pan of boiling water gently melt your wax in a bowl. Use a spatula to make sure all the wax has fully melted.

2. Add a drop of scented oil to your melted wax if your candle has no fragrance already.

3. The melted wax will be extremely hot so carefully pour the melted wax into an empty jam jar.

4. Add the candle wick into the middle and wait for it to set.

Touch

When it comes to feeling happy and getting that hygge feeling touch is very important. Find someone to hug or enjoy cuddling your favourite furry animal.

Memories

Get a lovely notebook and write in it each day with a pen all of your favourite highlights or if your prefer using the camera have your best in the moment photographic memories displayed around your home.

Don't grumble about the weather

Enjoy a break indoors on a rainy day with a book and don't grumble about the weather. Danish people are often topped top of the charts for happiness as they enjoy each day and make the most of the weather. If the weather is terrible make the most of the cosiness you can feel. Scandinavians also make sure they get outside each day for a walk no matter what the weather. It helps to improve mood.

Vitamin D

New advice on vitamin D from Public Health England (PHE), which says that adults and children over the age of one should have 10 micrograms (mcg) of vitamin D every day. This means that some people may want to consider taking a supplement.

Vitamin D helps to control the amount of calcium and phosphate in our bodies. Both are needed for healthy bones, teeth and muscles.

Vitamin D is found naturally in a small number of foods, including oily fish, red meat, liver and egg yolks. It's also found in fortified foods like breakfast cereals and fat spreads.

However, it's difficult for us to get the recommended amount of vitamin D from food alone.

Our main source of vitamin D is from the action of sunlight on our skin. During autumn and winter (from October until the end of March) the sun isn't strong enough in the UK to produce vitamin D. That means we have to rely on getting it just from the food we eat.

Community

When we think about some of our happiest memories it's often when we are with others. Many of the buildings in Oslo, Norway are designed with the importance of togetherness in mind. Courtyard gardens positioned in the centre of a building allow neighbours to socialise, eat and drink together. Through coming together those who are elderly or lonely are able to build up relationships with others, child care can be spread between neighbours and often a rota will be drawn up for social meals eaten outdoors.

Around Scandinavia there are many community gardens for growing vegetables and fruit too. What can you do to strengthen the relationships you have with neighbours? Could you make time to visit an elderly or lonely neighbour? Organise neighbour get together that involve cake.

Creating Hygge inspired interiors

Here is my checklist of how to embrace a bit of a Scandinavian interior in your home. Remember it's about how it feels just as much as it looks.

- Candles- Have a go at making your own.
- Paint the walls in white and have one feature wall in grey.
- Have an accent colour of yellow, blue or pink alongside the grey and white.
- Geometric lines in accessories and tiles.
- Soft throws of different textures
- Take the less is more approach with your home so organise and de-clutter. Everything should be simple and purposeful.
- Soft lighting with lamps rather than one big light
- Have plenty of books and magazines

- Light a fire
  Do you have a cosy reading nook? Maybe in the window or by the fire?
- Soft cushions of different textures.
- Indoor plants; palms, a peace lily or an orchid. These look great in white pots.
- Soft rugs on hardwood floors
- Carpets are often banned as they are seen as clutter so go for a natural wooden floor instead.
- Have things in your home that are special to you. It could be photographs of a family trip in a simple frame, a beautiful plant in the hallway or some fresh herbs in a jam jar on the kitchen windowsill.
- In your bathroom go for the softest fluffy towels, candles and the most beautiful smelling products.
- Ensure your kitchen cupboards have fine teas and strong coffee.
- Breakfast in bed with freshly brewed coffee or tea leaves.
- A wide selection of wine on offer.
- In the garden have a fire pit and seating to enjoy the weather in all seasons.
- Have the finest ceramics for serving your tea.

Early education for sustainable development

With many parts of Scandinavian having the lowest recorded light pollution in the world we can see how they care and nurture the one world we have. We can foster this care and love for our planet through teaching young children about sustainable development.

What is Sustainable Development?

It is now widely recognised that humanity faces urgent problems affecting local, regional and global environments, and social and economic development. The Earth's limited natural resources are being consumed more rapidly than they are being replaced, and the effects of global warming upon ecological balance and bio-diversity are well known. Rising sea levels threaten millions in less developed nations. The implications in terms of migration, increasing poverty, the supply of food and upon human health and security are extremely serious. The goals of the UN Decade of Education for

Sustainable Development (2005-2014, DESD), are therefore to integrate the principles, values, and practices of sustainable development (SD) into all aspects of education and learning. Sustainable development was first defined in 1987 by the Bruntland World Commission on Environment and Development (WCED), which argued for a development strategy that: "…meets the needs of the present without compromising the ability of future generations to meet their own needs" (WCED, 1987, p.43).

It has been widely debated that young children should have the opportunity to act upon and make decisions on the world that they will be left with as adults.

We can look at sustainable development in terms of three inter connecting pillars;

- Environmental Pillar

- Social and Cultural Pillar

- Economic Pillar

The best practice will involve support for all three pillars at once.

Environment

Depleting natural resources, increased greenhouse gas emissions, overflowing landfills and polluted waterways are a few of the effects demonstrating how societies have adopted lifestyles that have focussed on maximising immediate comfort and convenience at the expense of future generations. Rising sea levels are threatening many communities, and many of the people living in the poorest countries are the worst affected. These factors already have implications for poverty, migration, food and water production and health care. Unfortunately, already much damage to our planet has been done, and much of the damage is irreparable. As early years practitioners we have a role to play in offering children experiences, and in supporting them in gaining knowledge and understanding of the environment as it relates to their society. At an early age children can begin to develop the critical thinking skills required to make the sort of informed decisions that will affect the quality of not only their own and the lives of others around the world, but also the lives of future generations. Yet, historically this has not always been our way of teaching young children about the environment. Up until the last few years environmental education promoted awareness and knowledge about the environment, biodiversity, and the interactions and connections between people and nature. While environmental education has had a place in our education system for many years, the focus has now developed to a perspective emphasising sustainable development. This new perspective has a greater emphasis on equipping generation to take responsibility for making informed decisions towards a sustainable future by considering what is best in the long term. This no longer involves children learning about what has happened, but also about what can be done for tomorrow.

At Ireland Wood Children's Centre in England three and four year old children have been actively involved in setting up their own fruit and vegetable garden. Initially the children had looked at photographs of allotments around the world and looked at a range of fiction and non-fiction books on gardening for inspiration. The teacher noted all of the children's ideas, and the children also made their own designs of how they wanted their garden to look. As they did this, there were extended dialogues about where and what should be grown in the garden and how this could be achieved. Throughout the next few months the children helped plant seeds, bulbs and tree's. Later on in the year the fruit and vegetables were harvested and eaten at meal times and shared with family and the local community.

We all know from experience that if an adult has never recycled, it is quite hard to forget the wasteful habits habitats of a lifetime even when it is their intention to develop more positive values. For children who grown up, from an early age to recycle and care for their environment these attitudes will be sustained for a life time. In fact young children are capable of making even quite complex moral judgements. One concrete example is provided by Bates and Tregenza (2009) in a case study from Hallett Cove Preschool in Australia. They report on a four-year old child and her mother standing at the supermarket counter. The child is reported to have picked up an item and following a close inspection saying: "We can't buy these, Mummy…they don't have recycle symbols on them!" As Bates and Tregenza go on to observe, children are often seen as having little influence on our world. Yet here is an example of a four-year old trusting her beliefs and exerting her influence on her family, and thus, indirectly, on society (op cit, 2009). Many early years settings are already making significant contributions to education for environmental sustainability through integrating recycling and composting into their every day practice. Yet arguably, the biggest development that needs to be made in terms of the early years is to involve the children more closely in making decisions on the issues affecting their own lives and local environment.

Outdoor Learning In many Western urban contexts, during the last few years there has been renewed concern that children should spend more time outside. Outdoor education in Scandinavia has a high status, with the aim of improving physical development, and the child's connection with nature. Many of the Scandinavian forest pre-schools are built and run in secluded woodland, other settings provide regular access to local woodlands by bus. Throughout a typical day children have the opportunity to engage in child initiated activities and investigate the tree's, wildlife, and eco systems. The children are often encouraged to work in teams, problem solving and learning through direct hands on experience.

A discussion in the forest In the UK, forest school developments have also been extremely successful and have been shown to have made a positive impact on those children with behavioural problems and those that need to develop confidence and self esteem. Reggio Emilia has provided another international influence that has supported the learning potential of the outdoors. In fact in the Reggio Emilia model of early childhood education the environment is seen as the third teacher. Using the child's interests as a starting point.

The social and cultural pillar

The Swedish curriculum for preschools suggests that: "Children should acquire ethical values and norms, particularly through concrete experiences", but also "to support children's empathy and imagination in other human being's situation". This led the teachers in one Swedish preschool to exchange letters with teachers in Uganda, and to involve the children in the dialogue.

Children become interested in each other's every-day-life Two major differences were identified between the preschools. One was that the preschool in Sweden was municipality owned, and provided as a right for all children, while the Ugandan preschool provisions were being made by an NGO and places were available for some of the local children. The other differences were related to the inequalities in access to food, electricity and materials. These became the two starting points for discussions between the children in Sweden and Uganda. The children exchanged mails with photos and drawings, and every time a new envelope arrived there were new questions to deal with. The Swedish children asked a lot of questions from the start, but the project really took off when their teachers had a chance to visit the school in Uganda. They had successfully applied for a grant to do so. In their preparations for travelling to Uganda the Swedish teachers, children and parents discussed the very different levels of resourcing in the two settings and collected together a range of educational materials they could contribute.

Letter exchange The Swedish children also formulated many questions for the children in Uganda, like: "What is the most dangerous animal?" "How long is the tongue of the giraffe?" Many of these questions were quite odd for Ugandan children since most of them had never seen a giraffe. These questions drew the teachers attention to the need to address a range of popular stereotypes about life in Africa. The teachers took many photographs for the children in Sweden to look at. These photographs and the first hand accounts made everything much more concrete for the children. They could observe things in the photos and they asked questions such as: "Why are children eating the same porridge every day?". They also asked questions about the children's skin colour such as: "Why are these children so dark?"

The Swedish teachers thought it should be interesting for the children in Uganda to hear about the total darkness that people experienced in northern Sweden in the wintertime. But for children living in Uganda who had no electricity, they found it more surprising to hear that people were living with the electricity on all day. It was clearly realised how much easier it was to talk about cultural and human differences when they had this experience of having visited them. They also found children's were more interested when they could tell them more about their own every-day experiences in Uganda. The next step has therefore been for the Swedish teachers to apply for funds to bring their Ugandan colleagues to Sweden.

The economic pillar

The current level of awareness of sustainability economics is, by contrast, extremely weak and few practitioners currently working in the sector are aware of the multiple pillars (environmental, social, cultural and economic) that policy makers have come to accept as the major foundations of any adequate understanding of sustainable development. Yet young children like Charlie Simpson (above) show the potential for developing social entrepreneurs from an early age. It is for these reasons that we believe education for sustainable development requires programs that emphasise the importance of providing learning experiences for teachers and parents as well as for the children, and initiatives that encourage them to question how and why the issue of sustainable development affects every individual and community in a variety of ways.

Forest School Organisation

Getting outside in all weathers needs a little bit of organisation. Make sure each child and adult has the following clothes items all years round to make sure they are happy and comfortable to access the outdoors in any weather.

- Water proof jacket

- Fleece mid layer

- Waterproof gloves
- Water proof trousers
- Sun hat
- Woollen hat
- Wellington boots
- Thick socks.
- Sun cream
- Spare change of clothes
- Towel

In the entrance area to nursery there could be a space on a peg for each child to hang there all weather bag. It's important to think about space to dry wet clothing too. Invest in a clothes airer, a washing machine and dryer.

Forest School Activities

Use the natural findings in the wood to try out some of these activities;

- Make dens or a shelter for a teddy on a rainy day.

- Decorate wooden tree slices and hang them from the tree. We love using pens to draw a picture in the middle of them. Covering the drawn picture with tape and then pressing it down into a tray of sparkles. These can then be displayed from the trees.

- Make a fairy garden or leave a fairy door for the children to discover.

- Drink hot chocolate by the fire.

- Cook campfire recipes on the fire.

- Make a trail for your friends to follow.

- Land art with sticks, petals, leaves and foliage.

- Cook in the woodland kitchen with natural materials, pots and pans.

- Explore small world creatures and create your own stories.

- Use twigs and woodland finds to make a natural hanging mobile.

- Explore painting with the natural dye from the flowers onto old square pieces of white sheet.

- Bird watch

- Use sticks as magic wands to create spells.

- Bark rubbings with wax crayons

- Art work with charcoal and mud

- Explore branches by wearing gloves and peel away the bark with a vegetable peeler.

- Make leaf crowns

- Create your own flag for a den

- Sort leaves by colour with a paint sample chart

- Create a bug hotel

- Sort sticks by size

- Problem solve rescuing a teddy from a tree.

Camp Fire Recipes

Why don't you tell stories around the campfire and have a go at these tasty food treats.

- Cook your own bread dough by adding it onto the edge of a skewer and holding it by the fire. Add carrots onto your stick and dip into cream cheese for an extra treat.

- Grill bananas and eat with maple syrup or chocolate sauce.

- Boil oil the potatoes in salted water until tender (about 10 minutes). Drain. Return to saucepan. Add thyme and rosemary and olive oil to the potatoes, toss to coat and cool. Divide the potatoes among four foil squares and place one garlic clove on top of the potatoes on each square. Seal the foil. Place the packets on the grill over the embers and cook until heated through and sizzling, turning occasionally (about 15 minutes)

- Core the apple, leaving the bottom intact. Stuff inside with fried fruit. Sprinkle with cinnamon sugar and dot with butter. Wrap the apple in a double thickness of foil, twisting the ends to form an easy handle for gripping from the top. Place the apple upright on the coals. Bake for 12-18 minutes, turning occasionally, or until the apple yields slightly when pushed with a gloved hand.

- Drink warm Lingonberry juice

- Toast marshmallows

Risk Assessment in Forest School

With over hanging branches and trip hazards two of many risks associated with going to the woods you need to make sure you have a detailed risk assessment in place for woodland visits. This should then be checked by the leader before each woodland visit. Always make sure you take a mobile phone and a first aid kit with you in case of an emergency.

Talk to the children about the associated risks involved in working in the woodland and get them to create their own risk assessments that they too check each time. This allows children to develop their own responsibility.

Leading in the EYFS

As a leader either of a school, nursery, Foundation stage or class it's important that you lead by example.

Here are some thoughts on how you can value wellbeing and hygge.

- Leaders can provide staff with the tools to manage wellbeing at work. This can include leaders organising classes like meditation, yoga during work hours.

- Providing meaningful opportunities for social interaction maybe a staff craft evening or a local walk one evening.

- Promote physical exercise and healthy wellbeing. Have a water fountain, healthy snacks, making sure people have had chance to get a drink before a staff meeting.

- Do you have a sofa or comfy seating that you can meet parents or your team on where it is less formal than an office.

- Meditate with the headspace app. A few moments at the start of each day with your team. Even if you don't meditate get together and be quiet for 5 minutes before the children come in. It gives you the chance to plan your thoughts and actions for the day.

- In Scandinavia there are thoughts that if you're working long hours you are actually not good at your organisation. Work shorter but more productive days and don't stay at work till 6pm every night.

- Allow staff to carry out in the moment planning.

- Spend time in nursery and Reception working with the children without it being a formal lesson observation. Then make time to tell the teacher in the room something positive in a non formal way. For example I really liked the way you had created a cosy reading nook.

- Remember just like children do we learn through the processes of risk taking and making mistakes. Create an ethos of self belief and support.

- Work through the app Fit2teach.

- Introduce a new "thought of the week" board with a new quote each week.

- Offer staff a half or full day off as a reward for their hard work and dedication. This could be to get some Christmas shopping done or to plan their child's birthday party.

- Make sure as a leader you model equality and help with all the jobs in the Foundation Stage. This includes changing nappies, wiping tables down and tidying up.

- Send cards of real appreciation to your team acknowledging exactly what you are pleased with about their work.

Creating a Hygge office

Your office space needs to promote your own wellbeing and good health. Check that you have the following in your office;

- A green house plant

- Clear and organised space

- Natural light or lamps

- Soft furnishings like cushions of different textures.

- Your favourite tea

- Good quality chocolate for emergencies

- Inspirational quotes

- Your favourite mug

- A photograph album or frame of special moments to keep you smiling.

- A notebook that has a front cover that reflects you. Maybe its your favourite colours, a special place or an inspirational quote.

- A good selection of stationary.

Hygge through the seasons

Ideas of how you can slow down and recognise these every day moments throughout the year.

Winter

- Make home made gifts

- Print off Scandinavian patterns to use as gift wrap and gift tags

- Create your own wreaths, willow decorations and Christmas cards.

- Drink Lingenberry juice

- Popcorn and a film night

- Ski trip

- Sledging

- Crafting- sewing, knitting and paper craft

- Home brew your own beer

- Board games with friends and family

- Pastries for breakfast with freshly brewed coffee

- Make meatballs

- Make home made pies with gravy and seasonal veg

- Listen to the crackles of the fire

- Drink mulled wine or spiced apple juice

- Have a life connected with your loved ones. This might be through getting everyone together at Christmas

- Add fairy lights into jars along with foliage for a glow

- Brewing tea with tea leaves

- Visit a Christmas tree farm to pick your tree. Plan it well and you might find some reindeers

Spring

- De clutter the house

- Bring daffodils inside and display in jars

- Create a spring twig tree with collected sticks in a vase and hang spring flowers and Easter eggs

- Swap dark heavy fabrics around in your house and replace with lighter ones

- Bake

- Garden

- Go for a hike

- Take time to enjoy breakfast

Summer

- Make lavender soap

- Bake lemon and lavender biscuits

- Dry lavender out and put it in a bag to put in your drawer

- Buy luxurious ice cream as a treat or have a go at making it

- Sleep under the stars and star gaze

- Camping

- Have an outdoor dinner party

- Forage for berries and mushrooms and make something delicious with it

- Museli in the garden at breakfast time

- Freshly brewed coffee

- Go for a picnic

- Hike

- Visit the ocean at night time and see the light of the moon reflect on the sea

- Host a BBQ

- Take enjoyment out of burying your feet in the warm sand

- Read a book in the garden

- Take an afternoon nap

- Catch some live music

- Make iced tea

- Eat fruit salad

- Make a candle lit garden

- Have waffles as your afternoon tea

- Cycle everywhere

Autumn

- Put herbs in mason/ jam jars and enjoy the aroma

- Give children herbs to cut up, experience in the pestle and motar or even add to playdough

- Go on a woodland walk

- Make leaf crowns

- Collect Conkers

- Go for a crunchy leaf walk

- Forage for berries

- Bake a fruit crumble

- Cook a stew with homemade dumplings

- Search for the signs of autumn in your local area

- Bake pumpkin pie

- Make a carrot soup

- Read the story 'Stick Man' and then go on a stick hunt
- Have a hot chocolate and film night

- Take part in a Harvest Festival

- Leaf and bark rubbings

- Visit a Pumpkin Farm

- Decorate a pumpkin with glue, sparkles and paint. You could read the story of Cinderella and turn your pumpkin into something magical

- Make seeded fat balls for the birds

- Bike ride

- Make pretend creatures by decorating conkers and acorns

- Watch the Animals of Farthing Wood

- Make a mini autumn garden in a container at home. Fill it with moss, stones, leaves and sticks

- Have a family and friends roast dinner
- Create an autumn garland to hang up on your door

- Make pine cone hedgehogs

- Build a hedgehog home that will be ready for the winter

- Read Leaf Man, We're going on a Leaf Hunt and Pumpkin Soup.

30 Day Hygge Challenge

1-Buy a gorgeous new notebook and use this to capture this years Hygge moments

2. Go for a walk in the park

3- Eat luxurious ice cream

4-Find some furry friends to spend time with

5- Get up early to watch the sunrise

6-Have a no TV day

7- Write down three things you are grateful for

8. Do a random act of kindness

9. Make a happy hygge playlist

10. Visit a place with naturally flowing water

11. Look through old photos

12. Buy some new cosy socks

13. Light the fire

14. Read

15. Bring some nature inside

16. Bake a cake

17. Play a board game

18. Take a selfie to capture the days best moments

19. Make hot chocolate

20. Leave your phone at home and head for a woodland walk

21. Leave work on time

22. Have a drink with someone; coffee or beer. It's all about togetherness.

23. Change your phone picture to something that wil make you smile

24. Have open sandwiches (smorrebrod)

25. Light the candles

26. Use your actual camera...not your phone to take photos that capture your day

27. Contact an old friend you haven't heard from in a while.

28. Spend time with an elderly friend, relative or neighbour.

29. Make plans for March

30. Read back all your special moments from this year in your notebook and keeping collecting moments not things.

Photo Credits

Maryanne Scott Branding Photographer p2, Anh Nhi Đỗ Lê p8, Johan Lannek p9, Silvia & Frank p10, Aleksandra p11, Stocksnap p13, Foundations Nursery p18, Bruno Glätsch p19, PublicDomainPictures p 21, Carr Manor Primary p23, Ronnie's Pre school P28, P29 Roseville Nursery P31, Andrea's Childminding p32, University of Illinois P44, Cocoparisienne p45 Lukas Bieri 82 All other photos by Kimberly Smith

Bibliography

Bates, S., and Tregenza, N. (2004) Education for Sustainability in the Early Years: A Case Study from Hallett Cove Preschool, Australian Sustainable Schools Initiative South Australia.

Bilton, H. (2005) Learning Outdoors. London: David Fulton

Davis, J. (2007). 'Climate change and its impact on young children' Early Childhood Australia. www.eca.org.au

Dillon, J. Rickinson, M., Teamey, K., Morris, M., Choi,M.Y, Sanders, D. & Benefield, P. (2006). The value of Outdoor learning: evidence from research in the UK and elsewhere. School Science Review 87 (320), 107-113.

Fien J. (2002) Consumer Education, Across the Curriculum, UNESCO

Fjortoft, I. (2004) Landscape as playscape: the effects of natural environments on children's play and motor development, Children, Youth and Environments, 14(2), 21–44.

Gaiunt, C. (2017) Teachers putting three-year-olds into ability groups. Nursery World Magazine.

Garrick, R. (2004) Playing Outdoors in the Early Years. Continuum.

Grenier, (1999) 'The Great Outdoors' in Nursery World. 16th September 199

The Communication Friendly Spaces™

Leuvan Scale of Wellbeing and Involvement

Printed in Poland
by Amazon Fulfillment
Poland Sp. z o.o., Wrocław